Hero's Metaverse Adventure

Dr Dave Coin

Copyright © 2024 Dr Dave Coin

All rights reserved.

ISBN: 979-8-3256-5601-9

DEDICATION

For Zack and for all young explorers of the metaverse

DISCOVER THE MAGIC OF AUGMENTED REALITY
powered by Collectwin

1. Scan the QR code above, allow access to your phone camera and click on launch

2. Point your camera at the book front or back cover

3. Enjoy the Augmented Reality experience!

CONTENTS

	Acknowledgements	i
1	The Call of Adventure	Pg 1
2	Into the Metaverse	Pg 3
3	The Forest of Data	Pg 5
4	The Troll's Riddle	Pg 7
5	The Fiery Guardian	Pg 9
6	A Newfound Friendship	Pg 11
7	The Core of the Metaverse	Pg 13
8	Guardians of the Metaverse	Pg 15

ACKNOWLEDGEMENTS

Marius & Line Hammett
A.F.F.
Red Hat the MC
Sparklefart

1 THE CALL OF ADVENTURE

In the heart of the digital world, there was an adventurous doggo named Hero, known for his daring dives into new domains of the metaverse. He was small yet brave, with caramel-coloured brown fur for his head, body and tail and his face and chest a vanilla-cream. His eyes were bright and he wore a black superhero mask with white lenses that gave him a striking confident look.

Around his neck hung his favourite tag from a black leather collar, a shiny silver skull showing his membership to The Kennel Club, an exclusive corner of the metaverse where all doggos enjoyed eating the very best kibble and drinking the finest of gravies.

Hero's cozy den, located just outside the doors of The Kennel Club, was a place filled with memories, each a byte from his past quests twinkling like stars in his own personal cyber sky. He loved to sit and reminisce about his past adventures and talk about them with his friends, each story more exciting than the last. The walls of his den were decorated with trophies and gold badges, each one representing a triumph in a different part of the metaverse.

One bright metaverse morning, yellow sparks started to appear outside his den in the air above. Suddenly, bursting through these flicks of yellow electricity, a bright swirling portal appeared. The portal was a fascinating vortex of light, spinning with blues, purples and greens which made a gentle but deep humming sound. As Hero gazed up in wonder, the portal seemed to pulse with energy, creating a kaleidoscope of reflections on the walls and door to his home.

As if being thrown from the other side of the portal, a map unexpectedly flew out from it, floating down and landing softly at Hero's brown and cream paws. The map pointed to a wondrous area called the "Core of the Metaverse," a place of boundless connection. Hero became ever more curious, his ears pointing high and forward. He had heard legends about this place, a hub where all realms intersected.

With a wagging tail, Hero packed his virtual backpack, put his music earbuds in his ears, and equipped himself with a Wi-Fi compass and an antivirus flashlight—essential tools for a metaverse explorer. Hero also brought along his trusty tablet to document his journey, knowing that this adventure would be one for the books.

Hero felt a thrilling sense of anticipation. He took one last long look at the map as he leapt heroically into the portal and set off on his new adventure.

2 INTO THE METAVERSE

Hero began his journey into the metaverse, leaping across floating crystal platforms, each a portal to different games and worlds within the expansive digital sphere. The air was colder and filled with more humming sounds, but this time they were higher, glittery in tone, full of electronic data streams and the distant echoes of virtual fun. Hero marvelled at the sights and sounds, each world that seemed so unique and vibrant, his doggo senses stimulated unlike he had ever experienced.

The first world he encountered was a sprawling landscape of pixelated mountains and shimmering lakes. The trees were tall and blocky, their leaves a display of vibrant colours. Hero could hear the chirping of pixel birds and the rustle of virtual leaves as he walked. He took a moment to breathe in the fresh, digital air and enjoy the beauty of his surroundings. The grass between his paws feeling like soft lego blocks as he explored this new and unfamiliar terrain.

Along the way, Hero met avatars of all shapes and sizes: a purple astronaut exploring the metaverse worlds and stars and Marius the Tronbie, a green messy alien who was always tinkering with his gadgets. They were all sharing ideas and creating amazing tech and software in this virtual space. Hero stopped to chat with each one, learning about their meta worlds and sharing stories from his own adventures around The Kennel Club and beyond.

Hero then came to a puzzle platform, and he found a flock of pink flamingos with a strange third eye in their feathery bodies baffled by a challenging game. The platform was a floating island covered in intricate patterns and shifting tiles. With patience and a few clever tricks, Hero helped them find the solution together, their three eyes closing with a smile and a polite bend of their long necks thanking him.

Grateful, these pleasant avatars shared rumours of The Core's guardian, a fierce digital beast and gave Hero coded clues to help him on his way. Hero carefully noted these clues on his tablet, knowing they would be crucial for his journey.

3 THE FOREST OF DATA

Deeper into the metaverse, Hero entered a forest where trees were made of data, their leaves fluttering files and their branches streaming audio and video content. It was a mesmerising sight, with data leaves shimmering in the virtual sunlight like mirrors of brilliant bright glass. Hero felt a sense of wonder as he walked through this digital forest, the sounds of the chiming data streams were music to his ears.

The forest was alive with activity. Data squirrels scampered up and down the trees, collecting bits of information and storing them in their nests. Holographic butterflies flitted from branch to branch, their wings leaving trails of sparkling code in the air. Hero marvelled at the beauty of the forest and the diversity of its inhabitants.

With his antivirus flashlight, Hero scanned for bugs and other digital creepy crawlies, illuminating safe paths through the dense virtual underbrush. He encountered various avatar creatures, most of them friendly but some not so much.

Hero made friends with a mutant ape wearing a red hat with funny teeth and googly eyes who only spoke in rap, adding his musical songs and stories to his growing collection of tales.

But Hero also had to use his wits to outsmart the troublesome ones, one such avatar who lived in the middle of the forest and was waiting for him.

4 THE TROLL'S RIDDLE

As Hero ventured deeper into the Forest of Data, he encountered a particularly badly behaved creature—a metaverse troll. The troll was a large, grumpy figure made of code that had gone terribly wrong: corrupted code. His skin glitched with static, and his glowing red eyes narrowed as he spotted Hero.

The troll blocked Hero's path, his voice a deep growl. "Who dares enter my forest?" he bellowed, his breath crackling with static. "You shall not pass unless you can solve my verification riddle!"

Hero knew he had to act quickly. The troll's riddles were notorious for being impossible to solve, designed to trap travellers in endless loops of confusion, some never being granted entry to the forest. Thinking on his feet, Hero decided to distract the troll. He reached into his backpack and pulled out his tablet and launched an app, a debug tool he had been told to install on a previous adventure back home.

"Look here!" Hero called out, waving his device. "This is a rare item that can fix corrupted code. Maybe it can help you!"

The troll's eyes widened with interest, and he reached out to grab the tablet. As he did, Hero activated the debug app, causing the device to emit a bright flash of light. Once, twice, three times it flashed with a brilliant white strobe. The troll, blinded by the light, stumbled back with an almighty roar.

Seizing the opportunity, Hero darted past the troll, weaving through the trees and thick undergrowth. The troll's angry shouts echoed behind him, but Hero was too quick. He slipped through a narrow passage between two boulders that led him across a long frozen rainbow bridge and emerged into a clearing, leaving the troll far behind.

Hero finally emerged to find the data stream, a glowing aquamarine river of knowledge. The stream was wide and deep, its waters made of glittering code that flowed like liquid light. He crafted a raft from code snippets and set sail on the glittering currents, feeling the thrill of the journey ahead.

The raft bobbed on the binary waves made of transparent ones and zero numbers, the stream carrying Hero towards an echoing waterfall that whispered of The Core's power. The sound of the waterfall was a digital symphony, hinting at the wonders that lay ahead.

5 THE FIERY GUARDIAN

At the waterfall's edge, Hero encountered Scorcher, the guardian, a mutant hound made of code woven with fire, his presence a fierce firewall against intrusion. Scorcher's eyes glowed radioactive green, and flames flickered from his jaws. The air around him crackled with heat and energy.

The area around the waterfall was a rocky, rugged terrain. The rocks were jagged and sharp, their surfaces glistening with a metallic sheen. Streams of lava and steam flowed through cracks in the ground, casting an eerie orange glow over the landscape. Hero could feel the heat radiating from the rocks and the intensity of Scorcher's presence.

Scorcher's challenge was powerful; he conjured barriers of orange flame, creating a maze that Hero had to navigate with skill and speed. The flames roared and crackled, forming walls of fire that shifted and changed. Hero took out his Wi-Fi compass and used it to detect the safe patterns in Scorcher's firewalls, weaving through them with a cheeky charm and the confident grin he always had. The flames remained strong and continued to burn, but Hero's determination never wavered.

As Hero demonstrated his courage and clever mind,

Scorcher's fiery form flickered with curiosity, and his flames dimmed to faint orange embers. Hero inquisitively asked Scorcher what he was and Scorcher spoke of his creation, a guardian forged to protect The Core from those who might exploit its connective power. Hero listened intently, understanding the weight of Scorcher's duty protecting The Core and the metaverse itself.

6 A NEWFOUND FRIENDSHIP

Hero shared the adventure he had been on up to meeting Scorcher, showing him that the metaverse is a place of exploration and friendship and convincing him of his quest to find The Core of the Metaverse. Scorcher saw into Hero's pure of heart, realising he was an ally to The Core and not an enemy.

With newfound friendship, Scorcher guided Hero through encrypted pathways behind the waterfall, his flames now a positive beacon lighting the way through this digital expanse. The path was treacherous, but with Scorcher by his side, Hero felt confident and strong.

Together, they faced logic gates, solving difficult puzzles that tested their combined intelligence and will to succeed. Each solved puzzle illuminated the history and purpose of the metaverse, providing Hero and Scorcher with knowledge as they ventured deeper on their journey. They learned about ancient codes and forgotten protocols, piecing together the story of the metaverse.

The pathways were intricate and complex, filled with twists and turns. The rocky walls were covered in ancient glowing symbols and shifting patterns, each one a piece of the metaverse's history.

Hero and Scorcher worked together to decode the ancient symbols and unlock the secrets of the pathways, Hero logging this information on his tablet for safekeeping. The deeper they went, the more they discovered about the true nature of the metaverse. Until finally they saw a bright ball of light in the distance.

7 THE CORE OF THE METAVERSE

The light led them to an enormous cavern and they arrived at The Core of the Metaverse, a pulsing heart of light and energy where the essence of the virtual world came together. It was a breathtaking sight, with streams of data and light dancing and weaving across the vast ravine in all directions, converging in a magnificent firework and data wind display.

The Core was a massive, spherical structure, suspended high up in the air, its floating surface covered in glistening patterns and code. Hero and Scorcher stood in awe, feeling the immense power and potential of The Core.

The Core showed them a vision of true connectivity, a future where the digital and real worlds harmonised through the metaverse—a place that united people and avatars from all walks of life in learning, discovery and play. This was The Core's dream and Hero understood its message, after all he had experienced this himself with the friends he had made on his adventure already. The Core's energy, alive with so much potential, needed guardians to oversee its power, a role Hero and Scorcher were destined to fulfil and were glad to accept.

The vision was vivid and clear, showing a world where

everyone could connect and collaborate in ways never before imagined. Hero and Scorcher saw themselves as part of this future, working together to create a better, safer, more connected world. The Core's energy flowed through them, filling them with a sense of purpose, responsibility and determination. They pledged to protect The Core, teach its goal of bringing harmony and togetherness to the rest of the metaverse in a way that had never been achieved before, and promised that its power would only be used for good.

With their mission clear, the duo journeyed back through the metaverse, strengthened by their new purpose and the bond of their friendship. They knew they were ready to protect this wondrous and special place.

Along the way home back to The Kennel Club, they shared stories and dreams, their friendship growing stronger with every step they took together.

8 GUARDIANS OF THE METAVERSE

Back at Hero's den outside The Kennel Club, they planned how they would share their newfound wisdom and charge, and protect the metaverse's vast frontier. With excitement for the adventures ahead, Hero and Scorcher knew that together, they could face any cyber challenge. They mapped out their strategies and prepared for the future, knowing that their work was just beginning.

The pair stood at the door of Hero's den, gazing out at the digital horizon with the metaverse awaiting their protection. Suddenly, the swirling portal appeared again, but this time there was no map—this was an invitation. They looked at each other and nodded, their hearts again filled with thrill and adventure.

As they courageously leapt into the portal once more and into the streams of code and light, Hero and Scorcher were more than just explorer and guardian—they were best friends, ready to face whatever the metaverse had in store.

Their journey was far from over, but they knew that together, they could overcome any obstacle and unlock the full potential of the digital world. For everyone.

Hero outside The Kennel Club

ABOUT THE AUTHOR

Dr Dave Coin is a husband, father and creator in the web3, NFT and metaverse space

You can follow him on X/Twitter: @drdavecoin

www.herothedoggo.com

Printed in Great Britain
by Amazon